CRUISING WITH TONY AND JEAN

BY
TONY COLEMAN

Copyrights © 2025 by Tony Coleman.

All rights reserved.

I had just arrived home from the hospital. My Mother had been ill for some time and had just passed away with me at her bedside. The tears were rolling down my face. I had already lost my father and my brother, and now I was facing the rest of my life being alone. I had some good friends, but we were only together once a week. I spent the rest of the week on my own. I loved gardening and spent many hours in the garden with my memories of happy days. My long, dark winter nights were spent watching TV, longing for days when they were showing football. I also spent many hours looking at old holiday tapes on TV, revisiting happy days with my family. I knew thousands of people were in my position, but I still found it hard. I loved them so much.

I had decided that being alone was not for me; it was not how I wanted to spend the rest of my life. I had been told about dating sites but never thought there would be a day when I needed to use them. I was a quiet and shy guy, so dating people I had not seen before would be hard. I decided to leave a message and almost immediately started getting a reply from women who were lonely like me and were looking for a new partner. I replied to my received messages and invited a lady out for lunch. We talked and went out together on a few occasions, but I knew in my heart that she was not the woman I wanted to spend the rest of my life with.

The emails continued it was then that I received an email from a lady living almost 400 miles away in Scotland. She told me that she had just joined the dating site. I told her she needed to be careful when talking to men on these sites; they were not all like me. I told her that if ever she was down in Yorkshire, we could meet and chat. Then I got the surprise of my life when she told me that she came from Yorkshire and would visit her sister in a few weeks. We continued sending emails to each other, and a new relationship formed.

The lady's name was Jean, and she lived in a cottage on the grounds of Darnaway Castle in Scotland. Jean still had family in Yorkshire and would make many visits back home to see them. Jean came from a large family with brothers and sisters living in Yorkshire.

After sending many emails to each other, we decided Let's start talking to each other by phone. I used to start my call with Jean by saying, "Hello, Sunshine," and Jean loved it. We talked for long hours on the phone for over four weeks. We were both in love but had still not seen each other face to face, with Jean living in Scotland and myself living in Yorkshire. The slim chance of us meeting had been very rare. We both believe now that it was the Lord who had put us together and that he will keep us together both in this world and the next.

The journey from Darnaway Castle to my home in Castleford would take Jean about eight hours. Jean was a good driver, but I asked her to call me at every stop. I had known Jean for just a few weeks, but we had talked for many hours on the phone. Today would be the day we would see each other face-to-face for the first time, and I was very excited, looking forward to seeing Jean so much. Jean had phoned me on her way down three times and was not far from Castleford. I told Jean that she needed to turn right when she left the M62, but Jean was excited too and turned left. I knew she was not far away, so I phoned a Taxi to take me to where she had parked her car. Jean greeted me with a big smile, and I greeted Jean, as I always did, with "HELLO SUNSHINE." Jean and I were together for the first time and were to stay together until Jean died in August 2023. That night, we went out for a meal, and Jean phoned her best friend, Mandy, from Scotland to let her know she was safe and very happy.

I also spoke with Mandy and told her that Jean was in good hands. Jean had told me that after seeing my photograph on the dating site, she told her friend that it would never last as I was too good-looking. How wrong she was. Jean was beautiful, and everyone who knew her loved her. Jean was kind, funny, and had a wonderful sense of humour. Jean was the girl of my dreams, and I thank the Lord for putting us together.

It was time for Jean to return home after spending a week with me in Castleford. We had been very happy together, and Jean wanted me to go back with her and visit her friends. I planned to return home after two weeks but stayed with Jean for about eight months. The cottage Jean lived in was so lovely, and her friends made me feel at home.

Jean lived in a cottage just a short distance from Darnaway Castle, where Jean worked for just a few hours a week. Jean introduced me to The Laird and his wife, and they made me feel very welcome.

The woods where Jean lived were beautiful and full of birds and lots of deer. The area had many beauty spots, and we spent many happy hours visiting each one. Jean spent many hours painting beautiful pictures in watercolour and was very talented. Back home in Castleford, my neighbour thought that I had been kidnapped as I had been away so long.

Jean was an incredible watercolour artist, but her cottage had no room to display her art materials. Jean had to keep all her paints and brushes in a cupboard. I was amazed at the paintings Jean showed me; she was very talented. All my artwork was painting ceilings and walls. We both loved gardening and spent many hours working in the cottage garden. My job had been a gardener, and I had been lucky enough to do the garden of one of England's finest cricketers, Geoffrey Boycott. I used to collect Football and cricket memorabilia and was in touch with many of England's finest players.

One of my many memories was meeting Jack Charlton at his home in Newcastle, where we spent almost two hours sharing a coffee with Bobby Robson, former England team manager. Happy days. We never saw too many people passing the cottage, and I remember one funny occasion when Jean had some topsoil dropped off at the front of the cottage. I had just come out of the shower and was wearing a shirt and underpants. Jean asked me if I would take the barrow and fill it with soil. There is nobody, so you will be okay with just your shirt and underpants. I pushed the barrel out to the front gate and started filling it up. Within minutes, there came the noise of a ringing bicycle bell. I turned around to see a young lady with a big smile on her face. You were right, Jean. I said to myself, "No one would see me in my underpants." I returned to find Jean sitting in her chair, looking straight at me and just laughing. Jean had a funny sense of humour, and I had one, too, so we both saw the funny side of it.

When Jean joined me at my home in Castleford for a second time, I played an old tape recording that I had made singing the Jim Reeves song "Welcome to My World". Jean loved the recording and told me that I had a lovely voice. I was pleased to hear this, as no one had listened to my songs before.

Jean told me that I needed to record a few songs at the recording studio in Castleford. Later in the week, I made my appointment to visit the recording studio in Castleford for a two-hour recording session. I remember feeling very nervous; any thought of me recording a song was something that I never dreamed of doing. We arrived at the recording studio to be greeted by the owner, who could see how nervous I was and told me to enjoy it. I gave Jean my video recorder and asked her to record the songs. I was now very nervous and asked The Lord to help me make a good recording. The Lord never lets you down. My first recording would be "Precious Lord". The young man in the recording studio took me to the recording booth and explained what I needed to do. If I wanted to stop for any reason, that would be ok. They would start again.

Then something extraordinary happened to me. I saw Jean with the video camera in her hand, and the backing track to "Precious Lord" started to play. I was no longer feeling nervous; I was very calm, and my "Precious Lord" recording was beautiful. I could not believe that this was my voice. The Lord will never let you down; he was with me when I needed him. I was also thrilled with my other two recordings of "Send Me the Pillow That You Dream On." And my favourite Elvis song, "Loving You". When the recording studio owner returned, he could not believe that the very nervous person he had spoken to was the same person singing the three songs. He told Jean that she was right; THIS GUY HAS A WONDERFUL VOICE, HE SAID.

2009 CRUISE

In 2009, we went on our first-ever cruise together. It was with P&O sailing around the Mediterranean on their "Ocean Village" ship. We had a wonderful holiday with lots of sunshine and loved every minute. This cruise was the first we had ever been on; we both agreed it would not be our last. I will never forget the look on Jean's face when we went on deck for the first time. Jean was so happy. The cabin was very nice, with a good view, and everyone working on the ship made us feel very welcome. The meals were very nice, and there was a show every evening that started with Bingo, which Jean enjoyed. The ship set sail, and we were looking forward to our first stop, Tunisia.

We headed to the beach to enjoy the sunshine, and on our way back to our ship, Jean rode a camel. Jean had a big smile, and I stood there using the video recorder, just laughing. We also made visits to Monaco, Corsica, Palma, and Levarno. When we were in Corsica, we visited Napoleon's birthplace. Monaco was beautiful, too. The Harbour was full of Beautiful Yachts. We sailed into Naples, where we had a good view of Mount Vesuvius, and went shopping in Levarno. At the end of the first half of our cruise, we spent eating ice cream while looking out across the Bay of Naples. The second part of our cruise also included Genova, beautiful Monte Carlo, and Palamos. It was a wonderful cruise, and it would not be long before we were cruising again.

We enjoyed our first Ocean Village cruise so much that we booked again in early 2010. We booked a 14-day Caribbean cruise again on the Ocean Village. We were looking forward to visits to Antigua, St Martins, St Kitts, Dominica, Barbados, Trinidad, St Lucia and Tortola.

St Lucia

We had a wonderful time, and once more, the weather was beautiful. Jean made my day in Barbados, winning £800 at Bingo. We enjoyed some beautiful views, and the people in the Caribbean were so helpful and very friendly. We spent the following few months gardening and visiting friends in Scotland. Jean was such a nice person to be with, and I loved her so much.

In 2010, P&O told us the sad news that Ocean Village would be making its final cruise. Ocean Village was the first ship we sailed on, and we loved it so much. We sailed around the Mediterranean, and we had a wonderful holiday. October 21st 2010, it set sail on its final cruise. The cruise started in Crete and would end in Singapore on Saturday, November 13th. We were delighted to hear that we had received a cabin with a balcony to sit outside and watch the world go by. The first stop was Cairo, Egypt, before moving through the Suez Canal and onto Safaga and the Valley of the Kings, where pharaohs and powerful nobles were buried from the 16th century to the 11th century BC. From there, we set sail for Muscat, Oman. We enjoyed a wonderful visit, taking in all the beautiful scenery. We then enjoyed a full day at sea, sitting on our balcony before cruising to Dubai for a fascinating two-day visit. The meals on the ship were very nice, and if you did not go ashore, there was still plenty to do on the boat. Our next stop when leaving Dubai was visiting Cochin in India. Where we saw the iconic Chinese fishing nets that line the harbour, you could also visit St Francis church, built from wood in 1503. It is India's oldest European-built church. Jean loved it, and I wished we had the time to return there. After spending another day at sea, we made our final cruise visit to Malaysia, staying first at Langkawi before moving on to Kuala Lumpur. We ended the cruise in Singapore before saying goodbye to the Ocean Village and flying back home.

It was 2011; we were planning a Caribbean cruise. We were thinking of going in February 2012. I had been talking with the lady at the booking office on the phone and told her that Jean and I were looking forward to getting married that year and wanted a quiet wedding.

Then she surprised me by telling me we could marry on the ship by the ship's Captain and use our Caribbean holiday as our honeymoon. Wow, that sounds like a good idea. I told her I would talk to Jean and get back to her. Jean loved the idea and started to plan for our wedding. I went shopping in Leeds for a new suit, and Jean went with friends to buy her wedding dress, she was so happy. Jean was born into a prominent family; I had no family but lots of friends and good neighbours. Had we married in Yorkshire, it would have been a big wedding with many people invited. We wanted a quiet life, and getting married on our cruise was just what we were looking for. And we would also be on our honeymoon.

It was 2012, and we were cruising again, but this cruise would be so special. It was our wedding cruise in the Caribbean. We were sailing on the P&O ship Ventura and joined the cruise to Barbados. The next day, we were at sea before arriving at St Martin on January 30th 2012. We enjoyed a beautiful day in St Martin before sailing to Tortola on January 31st. After a full day at sea, we arrived at Catalina Island, where we had a wonderful day. The following day we spent at sea. The date was February 3rd, our wedding day.

The cabin crew was so lovely; they treated me and Jean like royalty. After breakfast in our cabin, Jean opened all our wedding cards, adding to our excitement. I spent the morning preparing for our wedding, looking forward to it, and thrilled at the thought of marrying the Lady I loved so much. There was a Lady on the ship to give Jean all the help and advice that she needed. I made my way to the room where the wedding would take place. The Marriage officer, Captain Paul Stuart Brown, was already there. A young waitress gave me a drink of champagne, and we waited for my beautiful bride. There was a slight delay for Jean and her best man as Jean forgot her wedding bouquet. Having done some singing, I recorded two songs for the wedding. I knew when the first song, "I NEED YOU", started that Jean had arrived. Jean looked so beautiful, but I could see she was very nervous.

The Marriage Officer, Captain Paul Stuart Brown, made Jean feel at ease, and the wedding went ahead. It was a beautiful service, and Jean and I were delighted. We arranged for a DVD of the wedding, and many photographs were taken with stunning views. Passengers were taking their pictures, too; we felt very special. We were in the Caribbean, and everything for our wedding was perfect. The second song that I recorded, "Croce Di Oro", was playing too and is now available on "YouTube". Later that afternoon, we decided to go for the wedding meal that we had booked when booking our wedding. When arriving at the restaurant, two waiters came out to meet us. We had just been married so I asked them for a quiet table with a sea view.

Follow me said the waiter with a big smile on his face. He led us both down a quiet corridor until we reached the end. Then we noticed that the room was packed and many balloons hung from the ceiling. We were being treated like film stars. I recommend couples wanting a quiet wedding with a lovely honeymoon consider getting married on a cruise ship. We spent the rest of the day in our cabin looking out to sea and reliving our wonderful wedding day. I turned to Jean and told her that Jesus had put us together and that he would keep us together.

Luxor, Egypt 25th October 2010

Later in the year, we decided to do a back-to-back cruise on the P&O ship Celebrity Solstice. It was a beautiful ship, and we looked forward to a wonderful holiday. The cruise started in Barcelona on Friday, October 26th. It will end in Singapore on Friday, November 23rd. The cruise was not too expensive, with most days spent at sea. Our cruise started with three days at sea before we arrived in Alexandria, Egypt, and we stayed there for two days. On November 1st, we passed through the Suez Canal before arriving in Safaga, Egypt, for 2 days.

the Giza Pyramids

We enjoyed visiting the Pyramids; what a wonderful site. That day, we also went for our lunch while enjoying a boat ride on the River Nile, we were having such a wonderful day. We followed this with a day visit to Aqaba in Jordan. We spent the next six days at sea before ending part one of our back-to-back cruises in Dubai. The second part of our cruise started with a day and a half in Dubai before moving on to Muscat, Oman. There were three more days at sea before arriving in Cochin, India, where we stayed for two days. After three more days at sea, we spent a full day at Port Klang, Malaysia, where we had a wonderful time.

Langkawi 11th November 2010

We arrived in Singapore at 7 am on the following day, where we ended our cruise on November 23rd. Sadly, I had been taken ill on the morning we arrived in Cochin, India, ending our chance to visit Cochin.

Cochin 7th November 2010

BACK TO AUSTRALIA 2012 16 NIGHT CRUISE.

On Friday, November 23rd 2012, we were cruising again. This time, it was a 16-night Asia & Australia cruise. Jean's sister Marion and her husband Allen were also on the same cruise. We were allowed to stay in our cabin, which we used on our just-ended back-to-back cruise. We stayed in Singapore overnight before leaving on Saturday, November 24th, at 6 pm. We stayed on the ship on Friday, the 23rd, due to a terrible thunderstorm with fork and sheet lightning, the worst storm we had ever seen.

November 25th

We crossed the Equator en route to Bali, Indonesia. After two more sea days, we arrived in Darwin, Australia. We had a wonderful day. We went on a bus ride in the morning to see the local sites before returning to the ship for lunch.

In the afternoon we went swimming, the water was so warm. We were talking to a lifeguard from England, and he was telling us about Australia's way of life and how he enjoyed being here as an immigrant. After returning to the ship for tea, we went out again to visit an Irish pub. We were sorry to leave after such a wonderful day.

There were three more days at sea before arriving at Cairns [Yorkeys Knob] Australia at 8 am. We saw turtles and dolphins yesterday and some beautiful reefs as we passed the coast of Queensland into the coral sea. We looked forward to visiting the Barrier Reef, where Jean hopes to swim. We booked our visit to Port Douglas to join our Catamaran, which would take us to Agincourt Reef. The journey was spectacular, passing more Reefs on the way. Agincourt Reef is on the outer barrier, only the coral sea after that.

On the journey, we saw a giant shark and were glad we were on a boat and not in the water. We had a great time on the Pontoon and went on the underwater Submarine twice, which was so good.

After a lovely lunch on the ship, Jean went swimming on the reef while I stayed dry, taking all the photographs. Jean told me there were beautiful coloured fish around her, making her feel amazing. On our way back to our ship, we saw lots of Wallabies. Jean told me she would love to return, but sadly, we never made it. After spending two more at sea, we arrived in Brisbane.

It was a beautiful, warm day, and we started by going on a tour with Marion and Allen to Lone Pine Sanctuary to see the Koala Bears and the Kangaroos. Jean got her wish when she cuddled a Koala Bear; she was so happy. Later, we got to feed the Kangaroos; we did not realise they were so tame. In the afternoon we spent a couple of hours in the Town Centre. It was so hot, so we enjoyed a nice beer and chips at one of the cafes in George Street. When we returned to the ship in the evening, we went to a show where we saw The Aussie Boys singing all the old Aussie songs.

What a great day! After two more sea days, we arrived at our final stop in the port of Sydney. We were all sad to leave the ship after such a long and happy time at sea. We arrived at the "Menzies" Hotel, where we stayed for the rest of our holiday. December 10th. We set off to find Circular Quay to organise where we might want to visit. We visited the famous "Opera House" and noticed our "Celebrity Solstice" cruise ship was still in dock. Sydney Harbour Bridge is a fantastic sight, but we will not climb it today. After a meal of fish and chips, we went out again in the evening for a walk around the town.

December 11th

We decided to walk down to Circular Quay this morning and got the Catamaran to Manley Beach. We saw schoolchildren taking a surfing lesson. We spent a little more time walking around the area before sitting down with an ice cream. We returned to the Menzies Hotel for our evening meal before going out for a short walk in the evening.

December 12th

Marion and Allen set off without us this morning as they went to Bondi Beach. Jean and I wanted to go to the zoo for a few hours before going to Watsons Bay for lunch.

Later that day, we made our way back to Circular Quay and then down to Darling Harbour. It started to rain, so we got on the Monorail and went back to our hotel. After our evening meal, we went out for our last look at Sydney.

December 13th

We had time for a quick look at the Harbour Bridge and the Opera House before it was time to leave the Menzies Hotel and say goodbye to Australia. After a quiet Christmas, we were off again. This time, we were going back to where we spent our Honeymoon in the Caribbean. And once again, sailing on our wedding ship "Ventura".

We arrived in Barbados on January 4th for our 14-day cruise with Jean's sister, Marion, and her husband, Allen. We boarded the ship at about 3 pm before eating our evening meal and looking around the ship. We were all tired, so we had an early night. The following morning, we were up bright and early. Today was a sea day, and we headed for Antiqua. We looked forward to meeting with Captain Paul Brown again this evening, as he married us in 2012. The weather was disappointing, with showers most of the day. This evening we were looking forward to going to the show. There was a tribute act to Freddie Mercury of Queen. We had seen him twice before on our cruises on Ocean Village. He had been fantastic.

January 6th

This morning, the weather was not too good again. We were in Antiqua and went on a tour of the Island. The weather picked up in the afternoon, and the sun came out. We went down to the beach, swimming, drinking the local beer and sunbathing. In the evening, after a lovely meal, we went to the show where an excellent comedian entertained us.

January 7th

We were in St. Martin, arriving at 7.30 am. We had all decided to go to Dawn Beach today, but the sea was rough when we arrived. We asked the driver to take us to Grand Case, a beautiful beach. We enjoyed sunbathing until 2:30, when we returned to the ship for lunch. Later, we went up to the top deck.

For the sailaway show, we had two hours of entertainment from crew members singing and dancing. That night, the tribute show was for George Michael. After another day at sea, we arrived at St. Vincent on January 9th. It was raining again; we could not understand the poor weather. It is our first time seeing so much rain on our cruise. The four of us went for a short walk, but Jean and I returned to the ship because of the weather. Marion and Allen stayed out as they had never been to St. Vincent before. After Lunch, Jean and I returned to our cabin and slept for a couple of hours. The sail away today was the British one, and we had a fantastic time. The young lads and lasses put on a tremendous show. We met up again with Captain Brown and spoke with him. St. Vincent is a beautiful island.

The following day, January 10th, we were in Grenada, and it was raining again. We decided to go to the beach, and the weather cleared, giving us a few hours of sunshine. They played my recording of "LOVING YOU" IN THE Hawian bar, and the DJ wished us a happy anniversary. The recording sounded great, and people loved it. Jean was so happy.

January 11th of 2013

We had a fabulous time today in Barbados. We all went on a tour of the Beautiful Island. Jean later went snorkelling with the Turtles. They were so beautiful to see, swimming around Jean in the sea, and she loved every minute of it. We called in at Diamond International on our way back to the ship. But Jean did not see anything that she liked.

We are going out in Barbados again this evening for a nice walk before returning to the ship for a Buffet meal. After two more days at sea, we arrived in St. Kitts and headed straight to Cockleshell Beach. The beach is less lovely than some of the beaches we visited, but the Island is stunning. We went swimming in the sea and had a great time.

Then we went for a long walk and had a nice Caribbean lunch. We are going to the show tonight, but Marion and Allen are going upstairs for an Indian meal. The following day, we were in Tortola on January 14th. We all went to Garden Bay Beach. It was beautiful, but the breakers made it difficult for us to swim in the water. Had Allen not been there, Jean would have been in trouble. The waves took her under the water twice and Allen lifted her out of the sea. I was on a sun bed and had missed everything. Jean went to the Bingo in the evening and won three games. We spent two more days at sea before we reached Dominica on January 16th. Once again, it was raining, but we hoped it would soon clear up. We were heading out to the beach again today; it is about a one-hour ride. We enjoyed a nice ride through the countryside, seeing how the locals lived in Dominica.

October 3rd cruise to AUSTRALIA, NEW ZEALAND AND OUR SOUTH PACIFIC ISLANDS CRUISE.

We left home at 3:30 am for Machester Airport on the first leg of our journey to Honolulu, where we joined the Celebrity Solstice on our cruise to Hawaii, Sydney, New Zealand, and the South Pacific Islands. We arrived early in Manchester and boarded an earlier flight to London.

We left London at 2 pm for the 12-hour flight to Los Angeles, where we stayed overnight at the Weston Inn just outside Los Angeles Airport. We stayed in a lovely room with a good view of L.A. from our window. We flew out of L.A. at 8 am on October 4th and boarded the ship after another 5-hour flight. Both myself and Jean were very tired after such a long journey. We settled in our cabin OK and went to a show in the evening. The local Hula Hula dancers were on the show. We thoroughly enjoyed it.

October 5th

We woke to a beautiful morning. The weather was excellent, sunny and bright. We went to Napolini beach. The beach was lovely, and Jean went swimming with the Turtles again; they were so close to the beach. We returned to the ship at about 1.30 and went up for lunch. The first person we bumped into was Anjesh, who worked on the ship; we had first met him on our last cruise. He met Jean straight away and then asked where Tony was. It was lovely to meet up with him again, we will be at sea for the next five days so that we will enjoy life on the ship. October 10th 2013 We spent five lovely days at sea, although we were surprised not to see any sea life. The weather has been in the 80s on all five days.

October 11th 2013

We dock into Tahiti this morning, and we will head straight to the beach. It is 6.15 am, and we are just cruising into Tahiti {Papeete} French Polynesia. The weather is great again, and we look forward to having our feet on the ground again after five days at sea. This morning, we had a lovely walk around this harbour town. The local dancers were here to meet us and gave us all the flowers. The weather here is scorching, and not surprisingly, the island has beautiful exotic plants and birds. We bought our usual fridge magnet and went back on board for our lunch.

This evening, we went to Deck 12 to see the Hawaiian dancers doing the hula-hula dance; it was a fantastic show. We left Tahiti at 9 pm, heading for Bora, Bora. October 12th 2013: Arrived in Bora, Bora at 7 am. The view from our cabin window is stunning, and these Islands are getting better with each one we visit. They are better than Barbados, etc., and they take some beating. Once more, the weather was scorching, so we went to the beach. The scenery is stunning, and so is the beach and the sea. Tony and I walked half a mile in the sea, and the water came to Tony's chest. A giant Turtle was about 10 yards from the shore, just basking about, so we swam with it for almost an hour. We could not believe just how tame it was. There were many people, but it did not bother the Turtle.

We returned to the pier, watching the local dancers before boarding the ship again. Tomorrow, we are visiting Moorea, another of these beautiful Islands. We are relaxed and chilled out, enjoying our time together on this lovely cruise. I love you more and more every day, Tony, for giving me this lovely life. October 13th: We arrived safely in Moorea at 6.45 am. The weather and the scenery were spectacular again today, so we decided to revisit the beach. The water on these Pacific Islands is so warm and inviting that it is hard to choose not to go to the beach. We had a lovely time again and saw lots of fish. We were treading water very near the beach when we saw this very long fish; we did not know what it was, but it was over three feet long. It was now boiling on the beach, so we returned to the pier to watch the local dances and do a bit of shopping. After that, we had lunch and relaxed on our balcony. We were very happy on this cruise. Love you, Tony.

October 14th

We will be at sea again for another five days and cross the international date line tomorrow, which means we will lose a day. We are heading towards Auckland, New Zealand. We will spend another day there and then visit the Bay of Islands, and we are both looking forward to it.

October 19th.

We arrived in Auckland this morning, ready to explore again. Because it is a large city, we will not be going to the beach. The weather is again lovely and warm but obviously much cooler than the Mid-Pacific. We had a lovely walk around the city, the buildings look great. We stayed out until lunch and then came for something to eat. We sat out on our balcony for the rest of the afternoon. We are setting off again this evening towards the Bay Of Islands, where the Treaty was signed between England. and the Mauri chieftains. Both Auckland and The Bay of Islands are on the North Island of New Zealand.

October 20th 2013

Today, we are in the Bay of Islands. Russell Island, just one of them, was the central Island where all the ships used to come in the 18th and 19th centuries. It is beautiful down here in every way. It's not as busy as it used to be, making it unusual. Tony, as usual, started talking with the two local Police Officers on the Island. The Policeman was from Warrington, England, and the police lady was from Scotland. Whenever they passed in their car, they would tell us where to visit next. They had been in New Zealand for eight years. We took some excellent video footage and visited where the Treaty between England and the Mauri chieftains was signed. The weather was warm again, and we saw many fish and dolphins in the afternoon.

We now had two more days at sea before we arrived in Sydney on Wednesday. On October 23rd, we arrived in Sydney at 6 am. The weather is scorching, but fortunately, there is no smoke from the fires raging in the Blue Mountains west of Sydney. This morning, we walked under the harbour bridge down towards the rocks. The weather is hot. Tony is taking some super videos of the bridge and the Opera House. We went back to Circular Quay, had a rest and then decided to get some shade, so we walked up to the Menzies Hotel, where we will be staying on our return from our next cruise to Figi via the Loyalty Islands and New Caledonia.

After lunch, we went out again to walk around the Opera House and enjoy the sights there. Sat drinking Champayne, which left me a little tiddly, but all in all, it was a fantastic day. October 26th 2013. Today, we arrived in Lifou, one of the Loyalty Islands, after being at sea for the last two days. Before lunch, we left the ship by Tender and received another Pacific Island welcome. This is another beautiful small island. The sea is so clear and for a long way out, too. We wish it could be like this at home. After walking around and looking at what was available in the way of goods, Tony and I decided to go on a trip around the Island. We visited one of the mud huts where many Islanders live and an ancient Catholic church. Love you loads, Tony. You're definitely a special gift given to me.

October 27th.

Today, we arrived in Noumea in the New Caledonia Islands. We received our best welcome ever. We were welcomed by the dancers and drummers, singing away as they all took part in their local dance routines. The weather has been kind to us again; it's scorching hot. We caught the shuttle bus into town. We decided to stop off at Lemon Beach and stay there most of the time because it was so lovely. We walked for almost two hours with Tony taking lots of videos. We watched a man fishing for sardines with just a tiny net, and he caught loads of fish. Another young man took his Labrador windsurfing with him; he was so cute. We caught the bus again and rode around the Island, taking in all the sights. We returned to the ship for a well-earned rest.

October 28th.

Today, we arrived at the Isle of Pine. It's 7 am, and the captain (Yannis) dropped anchor. We will be going ashore by Tender shortly. I cannot begin to explain just how magnificent the South Pacific Islands are. We thought we had seen the best when we visited Noumea yesterday, but no, they keep getting more magnificent on every new Island we visit.

We still have to visit Fiji yet, and I am still not sure what I will be writing in this diary then. I feel sure that it cannot be any better than this beautiful isle of Pines, with its gorgeous white sands. We went ashore this morning and decided to stay on the beach and do some swimming. The weather is hot, so we swam in the sea for about an hour. Then we took a long walk down to the end of the beach. We were the only ones to walk the beach full length. Afterwards, we visited the local shopping area and bought our usual fridge magnet before returning to the ship for lunch. In the afternoon, we slept and watched a bit of TV. We will be at sea for two days before we reach Fiji.

October 30th.

Arrived this morning and decided to go into town because Jean was not feeling very well. We did some shopping before going back to the ship for lunch. We went to see the Aussie Boys again tonight. We saw them last year, and they were great. Tomorrow, we will arrive in Lautoka, another Fiji Island. We arrived at the usual Fiji welcome. We could not visit the beach today because Jean had an ear infection. We spent our time looking at the shops before returning to our ship.

November 1st 2013.

We are at sea again now until we get to Australia. We are hoping Jean will be OK by then. Jean returned to the ship's doctor today, hoping everything would be OK, but it was not. The Doctor was concerned about Jean's eardrums and said he would not permit her to fly back to England. We were both stunned to hear the news; we had not expected to hear that. Anyway, the Doctor arranged for Jean to visit St. Vincent Hospital when we arrived in Sydney. We are both looking forward to returning to Sydney again, as it's such a beautiful city.

November 4th 2013.

It's 5.30 am, and we have just arrived back in Beautiful Sydney. The weather looked good, and Jean felt much better. Celebrity upgraded us to the Elite class on this last cruise, so our private guide looked after us when we got off the ship. She took us through the concourse [no customs and no waiting]. We went straight to our Taxi, waiting to take us to our Hotel.

After dropping off our luggage, we got another taxi to the hospital. Jean felt much better, and the Doctor said she was fit enough to fly home. We both pleaded with him to give us another week in Sydney, but it did not work. After lunch, we did some shopping before going down to Darling Harbour for one last view of this great City. Menzies Hotel upgraded us to a room with a view, which was very nice. Our holiday ended, and we faced a long flight back to England.

AUSTRALIA/NEW ZEALAND CRUISE 22 NIGHTS FLY/CRUISE 2016, February 10th.

We set off from home at 6 am to collect Marion and Allen from their home in Leeds and made our way to Leeds/Bradford airport. We were flying down to Heathrow on our 9.20 flight. We were due to leave Heathrow at 5.15 pm, flying with Cathay Pacific to Hong Kong. The seating on the plane was very comfortable, which was what we wanted for our 11-hour flight. We did not have to wait long in Hong Kong before we were off again for another 11-hour flight to Aukland, New Zealand... We booked into the Heritage Hotel in Aukland and went straight to bed; we were so tired.

The following day, the four of us went up the Sky Tower, which was very high, and we had great views of Aukland. We followed this by walking down to the Harbour and enjoying a nice walk. The weather was quite hot. February 14th, all four of us were excited we were about to join our ship. We walked down from the Heritage Hotel and joined our ship just before Lunch. We had lunch before going to our cabins together with Marion and Allen. Their faces were an absolute picture. We were so happy to see them so excited. We were all so tired and needed a good sleep.

February 15th.

We were all up and about nice and early. We were in the Bay of Islands. Allen and Marion had breakfast at the buffet, and Tony and I had ours in our cabin. We got off the ship and walked into town. The weather was a little misty and cloudy but surprisingly warm. Marion and Allen returned to the boat on the shuttle bus, but Tony and I walked it back. Tonight, we are all going to happy hour on deck three and then to our evening meal. We are also going to the show to see the Aussie Boys.

We hope to see both performances, as they are a terrific group. At the end of this cruise, we should all know the Australian National anthem by heart, February 16th. We were in Tauranga. We left the ship this morning at 9.30, and we went with Marion and Allen for a walk around Mount Maunganui. It took us only one hour, but it was lovely. Marion and Allen caught the bus into town. Tony and I continued our walk along the beautiful beach and returned to the ship for Lunch.

February 17th.

We had a lovely day at sea, relaxing in the warm sunshine. On February 18th, we were in Wellington. After early morning rain, the weather picked up, and it was warm enough to sit out on our balcony. After a lovely evening meal, we went to the evening show.

February 19th.

Today, We were in Akaroa. We got off the ship at 8.45 for a walk around the town. Akaroa is a pretty town, small but very nice. We walked to the front with Marion and Allen and bought my Kiwi ornament. The weather was not too good early in the day, but later, the sun came out to meet us. We are all looking forward to our visit to Dunedin.

February 20th.

Today, we are in Dunedin. The weather is cool and I am not feeling so good, and Tony has a cold. The sun came out about 10 o'clock, and we went up onto the sundeck. Marion and Allen went on a trip to Dunedin. Tony and I saw many dolphins when we were on the deck. We had a lovely afternoon.

After leaving Dunedin on February 20th, we went through Duskey Sound, Doubtful Sound, and Milford Sound, New Zealand. The views were spectacular, and there were lots of waterfalls. The weather was excellent, and we spent the day on our Balcony enjoying life. After two more days at sea, we arrived in Sydney on February 24th. Jean and I went to the Botanic Gardens near the Opera House. We went on a train ride around the park. The weather was beautiful. In the afternoon.

We went to our favourite place at Watsons Bay, where we had a fish and chip dinner before returning to our ship. After one more day at sea, we arrived at Melbourne. We walked around the shops and looked at the Melbourne Cricket Ground. The weather was warm and sunny, so we sat on our Balcony for the afternoon. After another day at sea, we arrive in beautiful Adelaide on February 28th.

Jean and I went for a nice walk along the riverside and saw many lizards, Ibis birds, and parrots. We then went on the Riverboat to see all the beautiful scenery. We saw the Oval cricket ground before going into the town centre. What a beautiful town centre this is in Adelaide. There are many lovely shops and cafes, but the best thing is all the live music. You can sit and eat your meal outside while watching the live band and singers. Adelaide is so nice that we wish we could stay for a few days. After spending three more days at sea, we arrived in Perth[Fremantle]. Fremantle had many lovely old buildings, one of which had been turned into a university.

We had a nice walk around the Town before returning to our ship for lunch and spending some time on our Balcony. After three more days at sea, we reached Benoa, Bali, Indonesia. What a wonderful welcome we received. The local band and singers were there in local dress, and they joined us in taking pictures. After a nice walk in Town, we returned to the ship for lunch. We passed many fishermen who stood up to their necks in the sea, trying to catch fish. We sat out on our Balcony after lunch as the weather was hot. After three more days at sea, we arrived in Darwin on March 10th. The Harbour is three times the size of Sydney. The weather was scorching, and after a walk looking in the shops, we sat down for a beer.

We went swimming in the sea before returning to the ship for lunch. We were in Darwin on our last cruise to Australia, and the harbour area is the best place to visit. After three more days at sea, passing lots of small Islands, we were in the Torres Straights. We had a Pilot on the ship in the Barrier Reef area. We arrived at Yorkeys Knob on the March 14th. The last time we visited Cairns,

Jean went swimming on the Barrier Reef. We had a wonderful time. This area has many Dolphins in the sea; it is a beautiful place to visit.

The next day, March 15th, we arrived at Airlie Beach, Queensland. It was just a tiny Town, and the weather was red hot. There was a beautiful beach with great views. The bay was full of Yatchs, and we swam in the sea. After a walk around the Town, we returned to the ship and had lunch. For the rest of the day, we sat out on the deck. We arrived in Brisbane on March 17th. From our Balcony, we saw a large Shark in the sea. I was pleased I was on the ship and not in the sea. After catching the shuttle bus into Town, we went to a Beautiful park with its man-made beach. There were beautiful Bougonvillias everywhere, looking very pretty. There were also lots of lizards in the park area. We went into the Town centre for lunch. There was a band playing beautiful music on Queen Street, where we stayed for lunch; the weather was warm, and it was Beautiful just being here.

We returned to our ship and spent the rest of the day sitting on our balcony. After two more days at sea, we arrived in Newcastle on March 19th. Noticed that there were lots of houses looking out to where our ship was coming into port. There were lots of people walking their dogs and waving at the ship as we passed by. We went to Nobby Beach, and our captain [Yanis] fired a cannon on the cliff top. We went for a long walk on the seafront and saw many fish in the sea. Newcastle is a lovely place to end your cruise; we enjoyed our visit very much.

THREE NIGHTS AT THE HOTEL WITH COMPLIMENTARY BLUE MOUNTAINS TOUR. FLYING HOME TODAY 23RD MARCH TO LONDON.

Special Thanks

A special thanks to everyone who has worked on "CRUISING WITH TONY AND JEAN." This book brings back so many happy memories, and it will always be by my side.

Thank you all.

www.ingramcontent.com/pod-product-compliance
Lightning Source LLC
Chambersburg PA
CBHW080853060526
44107CB00129B/618